MORE HEADLINES

REAL BUT RIDICULOUS SAMPLINGS FROM AMERICA'S NEWSPAPERS

COMPILED BY JAY LENO

WITH PHOTOGRAPHS BY JOSEPH DEL VALLE AND CARTOONS BY JACK DAVIS

WARNER BOOKS

A Time Warner Company

All author royalties will be donated to the Samuel Jared Kushnick Foundation, which funds pediatric A.I.D.S. programs and pediatric immunology research.

Warner Books, Inc., 666 Fifth Avenue, New York, NY 10103

W A Time Warner Company

Printed in the United States of America
First printing: November 1990
10 9 8 7 6 5 4 3

Library of Congress Cataloging-in-Publication Data

More headlines / compiled by Jay Leno : with photographs by Joseph del Valle and cartoons by Jack Davis.
    p.   cm.
  ISBN 0-446-39236-7 :
  1. Newspapers—Headlines—Humor. 2. American wit and humor.
I. Leno, Jay.
PN6231.N6M67   1990
081—dc20   90-39297
                                                      CIP

Cover design by Jackie Merri Meyer
Cover photos by Ann Summa/Onyx
Book design by Giorgetta Bell McRee

ACKNOWLEDGMENTS

I would like to thank the following comedians and comedy writers for all their help and assistance:

Jimmy Brogan, Steve Crantz, Jim Edwards, Jon Kleinman, Wayne Kline, Joe Medeiros, Ron Richards, Kevin Rooney, Marvin Silbermintz and Buddy Winston.

Also, Robert Jarrin for opening all the envelopes.

My editor, Rick Horgan, for taking my dresser drawer full of headlines and putting them in order.

And my wife, Mavis, for having to listen to me constantly ask, "Honey, is this funny?"

Jay Leno
Los Angeles, California
June 15, 1990

CRIMESTOPPERS

Men in blue, the city's finest, society's protectors. These are just a few of the names used to describe today's law enforcement officers—a hardy breed who take no guff, call 'em as they see 'em, and give as good as they get. The headlines you're about to see show why we can all walk the streets without fear, confident they're on the job.

CRIME: Sheriff asks for 13.7% increase

Okay, Spike, you've been hitting two houses a week. Let's make that three. And Lefty, I want to see twice as many purse snatchings. Let's all do what we can to help the sheriff.

From the "Your tax dollars at work" department:

Sex fund pledged for sheriff

County officials have pledged funds for sheriff's officers to buy sex at massage parlors in order to run several remaining sexually oriented businesses out of Bexar County.

Hey, why should senators and congressmen have all the fun?

Outlaw to announce
3 police promotions

Hey, you don't think these guys are working together, do you?

Mayor says D.C. is safe except for murders

Oh, that's a relief. I was afraid I'd get my car radio stolen.

High-crime areas said to be safer

Now, if we could just increase crime in the low-crime areas, they'd be safer, too.

Slow Driver Arrested After 4-County Chase

Los Angeles

The California Highway Patrol booked a motorist for evading arrest and other charges after a long chase through four counties that never exceeded the speed limit, a spokesman said yesterday.

It's a good thing he wasn't parked.
It could've taken all day.

Police blotter

■ Sent city police out at 11:38 a.m. to kick kids off the roof of a downtown furniture store.

Farthest kick gets free donuts.

No cause of death determined for beheading victim

How about stretched vocal cords?

9

Jury suspects foul play in Chapman death

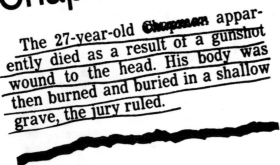

The 27-year-old ~~Chapman~~ apparently died as a result of a gunshot wound to the head. His body was then burned and buried in a shallow grave, the jury ruled.

We can't rule out the possibility of suicide.

Terrorist bought bomb parts at K mart

Attention K mart shoppers: plutonium on aisle 9...

11

Thieves steal burglar alarm

I wonder what they did with the Porsche that was attached to it.

Court rules that being a jerk is not a crime

ATLANTA (AP) — There's no law against being a jerk, a court has determined.

The Georgia Court of Appeals ruled that a former bank manager had no grounds to collect damages from her boss or an allegedly obnoxious co-worker, even if the co-worker was the boorish, obnoxious prankster that she claimed he was.

I guess we can all breathe easier tonight.

Robbery Suspect Mugged

A man stole $2,100 from a Brooklyn savings bank on Friday but was mugged as he made his getaway, so he immediately reported the crime to the nearest police station house, the police said. Officers promptly arrested the man.

You don't think this is the same guy who stole that burglar alarm, do you?

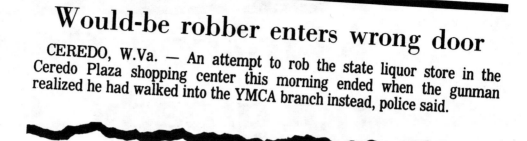

Would-be robber enters wrong door

CEREDO, W.Va. — An attempt to rob the state liquor store in the Ceredo Plaza shopping center this morning ended when the gunman realized he had walked into the YMCA branch instead, police said.

And yesterday he got mugged!

$3-million thief not greedy: Judge

Who says politicians and crooks think alike?

Wanted: A hangman who knows the ropes

Prison spokesman Richard Bauer says they really need someone who knows the ropes, because precision is essential. Otherwise, the prisoner could get hurt during the procedure.

Ow! My hair's caught....Ow!

(17)

Robber's description: Man, possibly a woman, definitely ugly

Hmmm, the problem is going to be interviewing suspects without hurting their feelings.

Son mistakes mom for bird, shoots her

A 50-year-old Roanoke woman was shot Friday in Bedford County by her son, who said he mistook her for a turkey.

Hey, these giblets don't taste right...

Woman Who Ran Over Spouse Gets 5-15 Years

Told doctors he was possessed by Mickey Mouse

What a shame... and on his fiftieth anniversary, too.

"Hey, I thought we were just going for a walk" department:

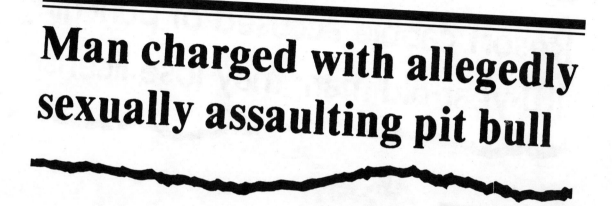

Man charged with allegedly sexually assaulting pit bull

Resort cabbie accused of punching 101-year-old man; may lose license

Combined with that pit bull incident, he *should* lose his license.

Capt. Pizza robbed last week; $1100 and cheese taken

On Monday, August 8, at approximately 6 a.m., the owner of Captain Pizza on Cambridge Street informed police that a window and the front door of the restaurant had been smashed and an unknown person or persons had stolen $1100 and three blocks of cheddar cheese, valued at $240.

Did you ever think you'd see the day when someone could take the cheese from Captain Pizza?

Man charged with theft after attacking pizza

A 24-year-old Milton man has been charged with theft under $1,000 because he smashed a pizza to the ground.

Police say the man approached a woman who was carrying a take-out pizza at the corner of Prince and Pearl streets. He then allegedly grabbed the pizza box from her hands, threw it on the ground and stepped on it. Although the woman resisted, it was to no avail.

Looks like they're out to get the captain.

"Slightly damaged goods: half price off!" department:

A **drunken-driving charge** was filed against James ~~████ ████ ████ ████ ████ ████████~~, after <u>he urinated on 11 boxes of spaghetti</u> in a 7-Eleven store last Thursday and then drove away.

"Hey this spaghetti tastes funny" department:

Police report in the Contra Costa Sun: "Police were called to an Orinda home after a 23-year-old woman became irate with her parents' nagging and threw spaghetti at her father. Neither parents nor the daughter wished prosecution, and all promised to contact their respective therapists."

Murder Charge Filed In Deadly Food Fight

A man, 18, was charged Tuesday with murdering his friend because the friend had thrown three hot dogs on their floor during a game, police said.

Imagine, if the man had ordered only two hot dogs, he might still be alive today.

Dismembered victim not a pleasant fellow

A 22-year-old Pittsburgh man who was dismembered and his body parts scattered around Allegheny County was a nice guy with a bad attitude, according to his criminal record and some who knew him.

"He had a snippy attitude," said ~~Anthony Michalowski's~~ former stepfather, ~~Walter Engel of Pittsburgh.~~ "I told him, 'You're going to get your throat cut someday.'"

"Ridicule drove him to crime" department:

At 6:45 a.m., the House of Erotica bookstore at 102 E. Charleston Blvd., was the target of an attempted holdup by a masked gunman. A silent alarm, however, tipped off police who arrived on the scene in time to apprehend the bandit still inside.

He was identified as Gene Wayne Vagina, 20, of ▄▄▄▄ Wyandotte St.

He's been teased his whole life, Your Honor...

Police recover stolen hamster, arrest 3

When burglars struck Immaculate Conception School in Bloomfield, their choice of loot quickly clued city police that the burglars weren't exactly big-time thieves.

Bypassing radios, typewriters and other valuable equipment, the burglars who struck May 7 at the school on Edmond Street made off with "Biddles," the pet hamster from the science classroom, and an aquarium containing two goldfish from the school secretary's desk.

Dog that bit 2 people ordered to leave town

The fate of Kirby, a Des Plaines dog accused of vicious behavior, could have been worse.

Cook County Circuit Judge Charles Loverde ruled Wednesday that Kirby must be sent out of Des Plaines, never to return.

How was this explained to the dog exactly?

From the "Winner of the sack race" department:

One-legged man competent to stand trial

LAWRENCE — The drifter who allegedly beat an elderly man with a hammer last month was found competent to stand trial yesterday after a 20-day evaluation at Bridgewater State Hospital.

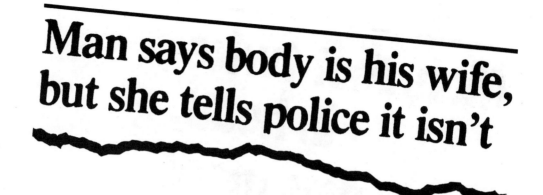

Man says body is his wife, but she tells police it isn't

Let's let the mailman settle this.

Man, shot twice in head, gets mad!

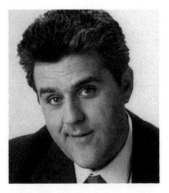

Don't you hate people who lose their temper?

Neighbors Say Sniper Not Very Neighborly

He was a quiet man, kind of a loner...

Campus killer to remain in prison despite apology

② SEEK AND YE SHALL FIND

Theologians tell us to find religion in our daily lives. Well, what better place to look for it than in our daily newspaper. Take these headlines, for example...

"He's back and he's not going to take it anymore" department:

Christ the King
Aims for Revenge

Purgatory tickets to remain at $27

Gee, I wonder if they give special rates for politicians and televangelists?

Sheriff and God Collide
At Church Intersection

Tell that to your insurance company.

Christ to serve
as presiding judge

I guess that pretty much rules out an appeal.

Pope to be arraigned for allegedly burglarizing clinic

Gee, donations must *really* be down this year.

THAT CAN'T BE RIGHT

This chapter contains headlines so ridiculous, so stupid, that
we feel compelled to reiterate that they were actually taken
from legitimate, non-tabloid newspapers. Is "serious journalism"
a thing of the past? You be the judge...

Londoner fatally injured by turnip

LONDON: Police are investigating the death of a man who was fatally injured after being hit by a turnip thrown from a passing car. The attack apparently was carried out by a gang who toss vegetables at random at passers-by. "It sounds very amusing but clearly it is not because a man has died," a police official said.

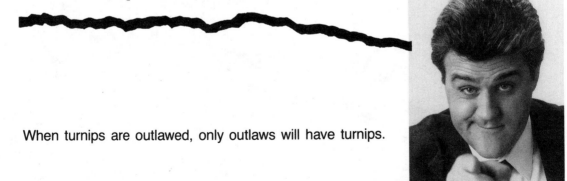

When turnips are outlawed, only outlaws will have turnips.

140 miles of sewers taped for television viewing

Gee, don't you think network television is starting to get a little desperate?

"Come to think of it, the *kids* don't say too much either—they just stay in their room all day" department:

Freeze-dried dog furnishes the fireplace

MEDINA, Wash. (AP) — Unlike most dogs, Puli the Hungarian sheepdog doesn't play on the furniture. Puli is the furniture.

Puli died in 1984, but his owners, Suzanne and Rob ▮▮▮▮▮▮, couldn't bear to part with the pooch that had been so much a part of their household in this affluent suburb east of Seattle.

So they had him freeze-dried.

Bland Music Competition Scheduled

Hey, is this how Zamphir, master of the pan flute, got started?

Blind workers
eye better wages

Is this the most sensitive way
they could phrase this?

Uranium 'theme park' proposed at Oak Ridge

Gee, I wonder if it will glow in the dark?

49

"Four days, three nights in beautiful downtown Chernobyl" department:

Dentists favor breast-feeding

Hey, it's better than having him
put that drill in my mouth.

When it comes to student achievment, how high is your high school?

You don't want to know.

"Gee, it's hard to believe the Japanese are ahead of us" department:

Schooling free but no room for students

Postal Service seeking ways to deliver mail more slowly

Has this been a problem?
People getting their mail too quickly?

Overnight, second-day mail will be delivered a day later

No comment.

Helicopter powered by human flies

Human flies look like regular flies, except they say (in a little voice), "Help me...help me."

"If you need any more proof that the Soviet threat is over" department:

Soviet 'biological weapon' was really bee poop

LOS ANGELES (AP) — The need to keep their offspring cool prompts Asian bees to produce "yellow rain" — excrement the U.S. government once believed was a Soviet biological weapon, researchers reported today.

**"You can't die yet. You've got six more car payments"
department:**

Car haunts owner from grave

MIAMI — Elio Mas, boss of the grave diggers at Flagler Memorial Park, told police someone stole his car, an '86 Mitsubishi Mirage.

Miami police found it for him. In a grave. In the cemetery where Mas works.

Shortly after 8:30 a.m., Wednesday, Feb. 22, 1989, a Sikorsky S76A Helicopter, leased by ~~Cessock Coal Co.~~ made an <u>unscheduled crash</u> a few yards off Rt. 19 at the Mansfield Rd. intersection in North Strabane Twp. Early speculation as to the probably cause of the crash was weather related.

Stick to the schedule. You're not supposed to crash until 9:00 P.M.

"Let's hope the Hillocks don't read this book"
department:

Surprise open house planned for Hillocks

Mr. and Mrs. Richard Hillock of Nevada will be honored at a surprise open house Sunday from 2 to 4 p.m. at Nevada Assembly of God Church,

Three ambulances take blast victim to hospital

Sorry about your torso, but the second ambulance got stuck in traffic...

TO SEAL - MOISTEN FLAP AND FOLD OVER.

DO NOT FOLD

STATE OF NEW JERSEY
DIVISION OF TAXATION
CN 274
TRENTON, NEW JERSEY 08646-0274

No comment.

④ A HOUSE IS NOT A HOME

Who among us is not touched by the plight of the homeless? Thankfully, concerned citizens groups are marshalling support for these urban wayfarers, as the following headlines show...

The Salvation Army is encouraging <u>home-less people to call home</u> for Mother's Day.

Telephones will be available to make the free calls May 14 between 4-5 p.m. at 423 W. Third South, in the northeast section of the building.

Nudist Group Donates Clothing for Victims

Humph...easy for them.

No Need to Kill Poor; They're Killing Themselves

Why not kill the rich instead? There's fewer of them and it won't take as long.

(5)

Everyone knows that the entrepreneurial spirit is what has made America great. And nowhere is this spirit more in evidence than in the wide range of products being offered today's consumers. You may not *think* you want that macramé life preserver or those neon dentures, but think again— there's a great big world out there waiting to be bought!

HAVE I GOT A DEAL FOR YOU

What greater gift than the gift of foot?

CUSTOM BUTCHERING
— Monday thru Friday By Appointment —
LOCKER BOX RENTAL

Home Killed Freezer Beef
Sold by hanging wt., Cutting, Wrapping & Freezing FREE
Front Qtrs. $1.29 - Hind Qtrs. $1.69 - Half $1.45

Don't let the grandparents in the last ad see this...

Yeah, but what about the disk player and leather interior?

TRULY AFFORDABLE EUROPEAN STYLING

POWER WINDOWS OPTIONAL!!

PEUGEOT

$5.00 VCR TUNE-UP

(Reg. $45.00 In Shop)

WITH PURCHASE OF ANY 2 LARGE SANDWICHES

We will clean: Video Head, Audio Head, Control Head, Erase Head, Tape Guide and Adjust Tracking and Tape Pad If Needed.

Big John's Sandwich & VCR Repair

Expires 5-30-89.

AB138/FMA

Here's your problem, sir. Your tape spool is clogged with mayonnaise.

All right,
here's my copy of the ad.
Give me one million gyros
and two with no sauce.

74

Gee, look at all the free stuff
you get for only $3 a month.
Imagine if you had to pay money?

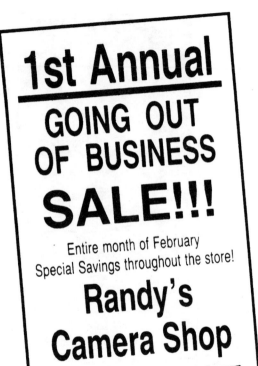

1st Annual

GOING OUT OF BUSINESS

SALE!!!

Entire month of February
Special Savings throughout the store!

Randy's Camera Shop

Gateway Village • ▆▆▆▆▆

Yeah, they've got great buys.
I went last year and
the year before.

I know rust is a big problem in *our* family.

SKOVAR
VODKA
1.75 LITER
80 PROOF

No comment.

First drinking...
now nude women.
What are these kids
going to do when
school is *out*?

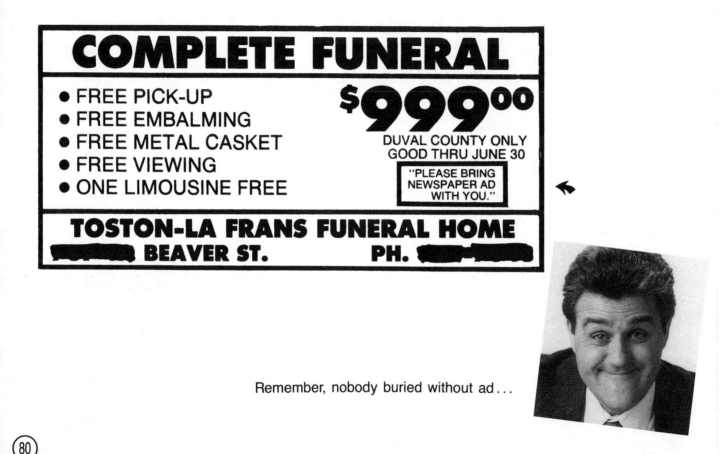

Remember, nobody buried without ad...

You Can Make Your Funeral A Pleasant Experience

It's All A Matter Of Planning

If you've ever had to plan a funeral, you know how many decisions must be made, all in a day or two. And that can be difficult at a time of emotional stress. That's why many choose to make funeral arrangements for themselves, in advance of need.

Now which one of these people is trying to make it a pleasant experience for the other?

81

Oh, go ahead. Treat yourself. You only live once.

(82)

MONUMENTS

$328

Complete, including inscription, delivery and installation at local cemetery.

ANDERSEN

1866 JOSEPH 1967

Choice of 16 designs. Full size 400 lb., Grade A Vermont Granite. Lifetime replacement guarantee.

Granite bases extra, as regulated by cemetery

Great for people who believe in reincarnation Can be used over and over again.

Maybe Mom will like this better than those power tools I got her last year.

FATHER'S DAY
at the
Oyster Reef

Our Regular Menu • 11:30 AM To 10 PM
Casual Dining Over The Water
By The Boats

Complimentary Glass Of Champagne
And A <u>Hooker</u> For Dad

FOR RESERVATIONS, ~~████████~~ **OAKLAND**
~~████████~~ **EMBARCADERO**

Why do I think this place is booked up already?

What better gift this holiday season: the gift of lead.

BON APPÉTIT!

Tired of that same old diet of tofu and oat bran? Well, here's some good eatin' that's sure to please the palate (and, we hear, low in cholesterol, too)...

ISU makes cow chips latest snack

ISU adds beef to corn chips to make a light, crunchy snack

The market for beefed up corn chips has a very bullish outlook, according to one Iowa State researcher.

██████ █████, professor of animal science, said the U.S. snack food market is ready for ISU's latest culinary development — the beef-corn snack chip.

Uh, no thanks. I'm trying to cut down.

Ants take a long time to cook in microwave

But well worth the wait.

89

Do neat stuff like drinking sewer lice, teachers urged

Make a worm farm. Implode an aluminum can. Drink sewer lice. Carve rubber stamps out of erasers. Let pill bugs race. Launch a rocket.

Those stunts may read like a list penned by a vengeful delinquent, but they're actually a few teaching tools about **30** science teachers from around the state will explain during "Science on Saturday" from 8 a.m. to 3:30 p.m. Saturday at Memorial High

Here's an argument against tenure.

US says insect parts, rat hair are OK in food

Washington, D.C. —AP— Insect parts, rodent hairs and maggots don't sound appetizing, but when tossed with a salad, churned up in tomato sauce or baked in bread they're not bad at all, the government says.

But how do they taste with cow chips?

Nothing fishy about this

Spam sushi's a hit at S.J. restaurant

You wonder why more and more people are eating at home?

Pet cooking contest coming to Highland

More than $1,000 in prizes will be at stake when Pet Inc. and the City of Highland sponsor the Pet Palate Pleasers 2nd Annual Cooking Contest.

Uh, excuse me, can I use your dog basting brush?

HAMPTON - <u>The Hampton United Methodist Church</u> will sponsor a Harvest Supper on Saturday, October 1. The dinner will be served in two seatings: one at 5 p.m. and one at 6:30 p.m. Reservations are required and may be made by contacting the church office at 926-2702.

➡ <u>The menu for the evening will be a traditional New England boiled sinner,</u> rolls, homemade apple pie, coffee, tea and cider. Admission is - Adults $6.75, children age 6 to 11 - $3.75, children under the age of 6 are admitted free.

Boy, and you thought Southern Baptists were strict.

Preview of Events

Chicken Dinner

Hibben United Methodist Church will sponsor a barbecue chicken dinner on Saturday, March 2, from 4 to 7 p.m. at the church on Coleman Boulevard. Takeouts will be available. Adults, $4.50, children 12 and under, $2.50, children under five free if eaten in dining room.

Gosh, I'm hungry.
Hand me that plate
of preschoolers, will you?

95

$9.95?! I can eat kids
for free at the
United Methodist Church.

School lunch menu . . .

Monday, Dec. 5
Baked chicken nuggets w. sweet & sour sauce, oven fried potatoes, carrots & celery stix, chilled pineapple tid-bits, milk

Tuesday, Dec. 6
Chilled fruit juice, grilled cheeseburger on a roll w. ketchup, pickles & chips, chilled pears, milk

Wednesday, Dec. 7
Submarine sandwich on French Bread w. sliced meats, cheese, lettuce, tomatoes & pickles, oven fried potatoes, strawberry jello w. topping, milk

Thursday, Dec. 8
Cup of children w. rice soup, cheese/tomato pizza, vegetable salad w. dressing, chilled peaches, milk

Friday, Dec. 9
Roast turkey w. gravy, whipped potatoes, sliced carrots & peas, cranberry sauce, bread & butter, chilled fruit cocktail, milk

The United Methodist Church is still the best deal in town.

97

7

If you thought death was the end of your fiduciary responsibilities, that you could rest in peace and not have to worry about keeping up appearances, think again...

THE TROUBLE WITH BEING DEAD

City wants Dead to pay for cleanup

It's about time. They've been lying around long enough.

Saints Rest Cemetery's
Annual Third Sunday in August Homecoming
August 20, 1989 Come as early as you like - Stay as long as you like Lunch at noon - Business Meeting After Lunch - Singing in the Church Come enjoy the day with us.

Wouldn't Halloween be a more appropriate time for this event?

Teacher Dies; Board Accepts His Resignation

Normally we wouldn't, but I guess this time it's okay.

Man reports wife's death —after game

Police questioning delay following fatal shooting

A Clayton County man told police his wife shot herself in the head after an argument Sunday, but he decided to go to his mother-in-law's house to watch the Super Bowl instead of reporting her death, officers said.

Yeah . . . so?

103

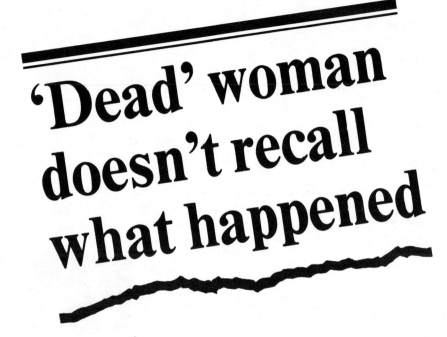

'Dead' woman doesn't recall what happened

All right, we're going to go over it one more time,
and I'll sit here all night if I have to...

Mortuary adds drive-through

Mourners pay their final respects without having to leave their cars

Gee, I wonder if this is in L.A.?

You can still bury grandpa out back

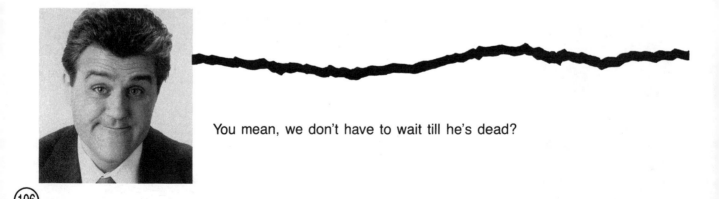

You mean, we don't have to wait till he's dead?

New Stupid Way to Die Discovered

DANBURY, N.H. — An empty beer keg thrown onto a campfire exploded yesterday, killing a man at his birthday party in the second such death reported this month.

It's amazing how many new discoveries are made every day.

Woman Leaps To Death at Shea Stadium

New York

A woman climbed to the top of the right-field foul pole at empty Shea Stadium yesterday and jumped 120 feet to her death on the playing field, police said.

The woman, estimated to be between 30 and 40 years old, landed in what would be foul territory during a game. She was pronounced dead at the scene.

A foul? So she may have to jump again.

Man 'mooned' train before being struck

LIGONIER — Noble County police and the county coroner have yet to identify a man who was struck and killed by a Conrail train early Monday after he dropped his pink shorts and "mooned" the train.

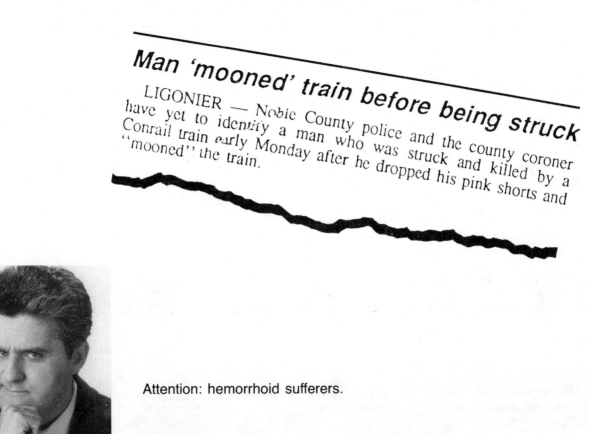

Attention: hemorrhoid sufferers.

2 Rich Tennesseans' Deaths Pump $9 Into State Coffers

Oh, sure, the $9 looks good now, but once you deduct inheritance taxes and lawyers' fees...

For many, it's the favorite part of the evening newspaper—
the section where you can get a line on that '65 Buick you've
been wanting, check if they're any new listings for unskilled
laborers, or look for a buyer for those 30 metric tons of
solid toxic waste sitting behind your asbestos factory. What
are we talking about? Well, the classifieds, of course...

CLASSIFY THIS, WILL YOU?

**Thinking about
Selling Those No Longer
Needed Items?**

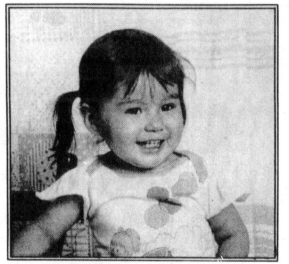

**Give The A-J Classifieds
A Try At A Price
You Can Afford.**

DIVORCE SALE 1444 LOVERS LANE, April 29
8 AM to 5 PM - Furniture & Misc.

Some people just can't
handle the pressure, I guess.

---- ---- ---- ---- ---- ---- ---- ----

USED REAR ENDS
**For most cars and light trucks,
$65 or $149.95 Installed.**

And I'm sure it was owned by a little old lady
who only sat on it in church on Sunday...

TRADE dental work for car or anything
of value. 284-0272

How about a used rear end?

GRANDMOTHER WILL babysit 205 year old in her Stuart home.

205 year olds? Don't these kids have older brothers and sisters to take care of them?

PERSON to help wash windows. Send resume to P.O. Box ███, Williamsport, PA ████

After I graduated from Harvard, I went to the Wharton School of Business—plus I own my own rag.

RECEPTIONIST/LAW FIRM
$189,000 YR + BONUS

Greet important visitors, schedule appointments & answer phones on beautiful executive floor of top Chicago client law firm. 9 to 5; 5 days. Must have excellent personality, nice appearance & work well in a fast paced atmosphere. 100% public contact.

$189,000 a year...hmmm, but what about the bonus?

CHICKEN SEXER. To separate chicks by sex using the vent method to examine for presence or absence of male eminence. Require 1 year experience.

Do you think this is how the Colonel got started?

Alaska Airlines...swimming....
It's not the swimming that bothers me, it's breaking through that ice.

F96. Love dogs? Write to this lonely widow. She is 49, 150lbs, changeable eyes, financially secure, high morals, non-drinker, non-drugs. MAF40603B

Is this the *best* way to phrase your ad?

Courts

COUNTY COURT-AT-LAW NO. 1
Judge Weldon Copeland, presiding
Criminal Docket
Dispositions
1/11/89

Roger Dale ████, guilty of overweight. Fined $113.50.

Guilty of being overweight?!
Good thing he wasn't wearing
plaid pants and white shoes—
he could've gotten jail time.

ORDER FOR HEARING
Case No. N/C 240

In the Matter of a Change of Name for:
**HANG HANG VANG
BEE VANG
KONG M. VANG
KABOA VANG
PHENG VANG
AMY LYNN VANG
DANNY VANG**

It appearing from the petition of Ge Vang Khang and Hang Hang Vang that they desire to make the following name changes:

Hang Hang Vang to Hang Vang Khang; Bee Vang to Bee Vang Khang; Kong M. Vang to Kongmeng Vang Khang; Kabao Vang to Kabao Vang Khang; Pheng Vang to Pheng Vang Khang; Amy Lynn Vang to Amy Vang Khang; Danny Vang to Danny Vang Khang.

NOW, THEREFORE, on motion of Crowns, Midthun, Metcalf & Quinn S.C., by Ellen K. Schroeder, attorneys for said petitioners;

Say this one three times, real fast . . .

You get what you pay for.

Man stuck on toilet; stool suspected

Once-sagging cloth diaper industry saved by full dumps

Environmental concerns and other factors are creating a "substantial shift back to cloth diapers," the president of a diaper service which serves Terre Haute said Friday.

Moorpark residents enjoy a communal dump

All good couches must be laid to rest — in a place other than the backyard or the garage — sooner or later.

So must busted chairs and broken washing machines.

And several items such as these were finally thrown away Saturday during Moorpark's Neighborhood Cleanup Program.

Oshkosh sued for injury over runaway outhouse

An Oshkosh man is suing the city of Oshkosh for injuries sustained when he was hit by a runaway outhouse during last summer's Sawdust Daze celebration.

129

Market in urine samples expected to grow

Hemorrhoids inspire respectful hindsight

Circumcisions Cut Back

STOP THE PRESSES!

We live in an exciting era—one rife with discoveries, breakthroughs, and insights. Why, it seems hardly a day passes without some important finding being published. Take these headlines, for example...

Blow to head is common cause of brain injury

Duh . . .

Low pay reason for poverty, study says

Double duh...

Experts Are Sure the Dow Will Either Rise or Decline

Boy, business forecasting is an exact science, isn't it?

"You mean it won't drain out the top?" department:

Drain plug located at bottom

July 4, 1776, Was 'A Turning Point In History,' President Says

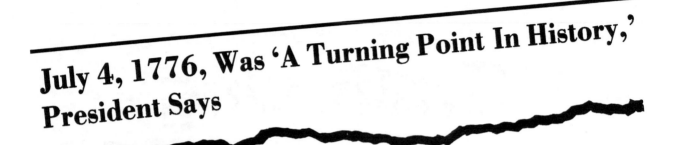

Who says politicians are afraid to go out on a limb?

Don't leave kids alone with molester

Am I glad I read the paper today.

Radioactive Dump Could Be Hazard

Yeah, but only for the next three million years.

Health Tip

Studies indicate fat intake affects obesity

Thanks for the tip.

Storm delayed by bad weather

Another picnic ruined.

Married women can enter the Mrs. Arizona pageant

Then single women should be able to enter
the Miss Arizona pageant.

Unfair. Men should be able to find out if they're pregnant, too.

FORBIDDEN FRUIT

We've all seen it—that come-hither headline that taunts with its innuendo. The kind that has you craning your neck to read the paper of the person in front of you, sure that a certain naughty subject is about to be discussed. Somehow, though, like that officemate who gives you a suggestive wink at the coffee machine, it always seems to promise more than it delivers...

Vets called in to cool down duck sex orgy

HOBART, Australia (AFP) — Authorities had to drug 16 sex-crazed drakes who were drowning their lady-love ducks in aquatic orgies on Launceston City Park pond.

"Their heavy love-making in the pond was just too much for the little ducks and the weight of numbers drowned them," said a Launceston city council spokesman.

And you thought Hef's was wild.

State to punish duck violators

You've got to be pretty sick to violate a duck.

Sex with weeds may be hurting plant genetics

I've heard of people talking to their plants,
but this is ridiculous.

Sperm-donor project may boost chicken industry

What? No dinner and movie first?

Bush orders Army troops to U.S. Virgins

Gee, kinda makes you want to put on a uniform, doesn't it?

"Why Congress is fighting to keep our bases open" department:

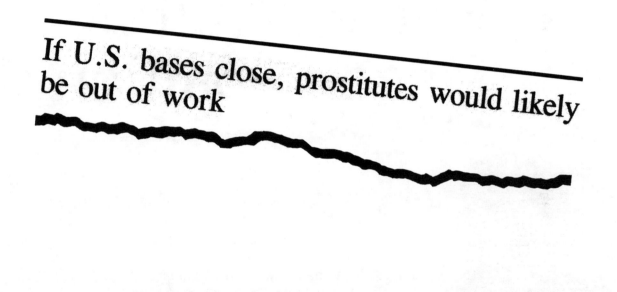

If U.S. bases close, prostitutes would likely be out of work

Hooker Quits
Mason Position

I guess it can be really rough on the elbows.

Hooker leaves partners hanging

You think this has anything to do with the Mason position?

Horney man indicted on sex charge

If people are going to jail for this,
no congressman is safe.

If Voters Approve, Boys Town Will Buy Orphanage With Girls

Party… party… party…

And the thing I like about it, it's so subtle.

Wanted: Women To Test New Condom

I've heard of phony ways to meet women but this one takes the cake.

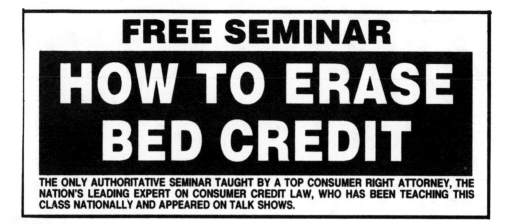

FREE SEMINAR

HOW TO ERASE BED CREDIT

THE ONLY AUTHORITATIVE SEMINAR TAUGHT BY A TOP CONSUMER RIGHT ATTORNEY, THE NATION'S LEADING EXPERT ON CONSUMER CREDIT LAW, WHO HAS BEEN TEACHING THIS CLASS NATIONALLY AND APPEARED ON TALK SHOWS.

Good idea, who hasn't had a few of those they wouldn't mind erasing?

San Luis Obispo

Police were called Sunday night to the Economy Motel by a man having trouble getting his wife out of a pair of handcuffs.

<u>No other information was available.</u>

★ ★ ★

No other information is needed.

Good Ol' Days

April 1, 1981

Amy Marie was born to Randy and Robin and Jessica Faulk on March 27.

Ah...life on the commune.

PHOTO FOUL-UPS

By far, my favorite journalistic gaffes are weird photo/headline juxtapositions that, though unintentional, conjure up frightening thoughts. See if these foul-ups don't give you a few shudders...

New drug brightens aging brain

WASHINGTON (AP) — Brains dulled by age may be restored to the quick brightness of youth by a new drug developed for treatment of stroke, Chicago researchers report in a study published today.

President George Bush

Hey, do you think the guy who positioned this photo is a Democrat?

COFFEYVILLE JOURNAL

Quayle dodges shots off trail

Sacramento's
Newest Luxury Hotel

Riverboat Delta King

Hmmm, I wonder
if rooms below
the waterline
are cheaper?

Rabbits Nibbling Away Big Chunks of Australia

CANBERRA, Australia—This country is at war with 200 million rabbits nibbling their way at great expense across vast tracts of land.

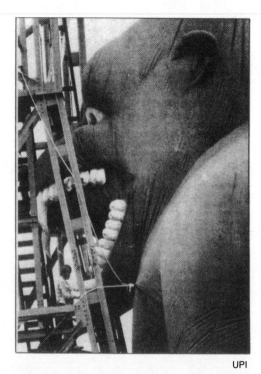

Inflated appearance—Worker inflates a 2,000-pound, 70-foot-tall replica of King Kong attached to 300-foot-high observation tower at Six Flags Over Texas amusement park near Dallas.

Where's Crocodile Dundee when you need him?

Firefighting tactics in fatal blaze will get close look

I hope so. The savings in gas and oil don't begin to make up for the peanut bills.

From the "Bill, we think you'll be better off behind the grill instead of working the customer window" department:

Handicapped find job help

Biology instructor David Sutton adjusted an octopus outfit worn by Tim Shipley, 17

Roaming Back Roads of Romania by Rental Car

BUCHAREST, Romania—When a friend and I booked our 10-day Romania self-drive package it seemed too good to be true: rental car with unlimited mileage, insurance, even coupons for 70 liters of gas, hotels, two meals a day, visa, transfers and assistance on arrival and departure. All for just over $600 each.

JOYCE M. DALTON

But do you get unlimited mileage?

Secret shuttle flight has been flawless

These are the possible landing sites for the shuttle.

ASSOCIATED PRESS

Are these *really* the possible landing sites for the shuttle?
It looks like the parking lot is full.

"Funny, there was water here yesterday" department:

THE ARIZONA DAILY STAR

Travel plans changed

Although Hurricane Gilbert is expected to smash into the Gulf Coast about 1,000 miles southeast of Tucson, it is affecting some traveling Tucsonans.

From the "I think it's just mist" department:

Officials Deny Presence of Toxic Flames

SALT LAKE TRIBUNE

171

ALEX BRANDON/ARKANSAS DEMOCRAT

PROPANE BLAST — This is one of two homes destroyed in a Tuesday afternoon blast in Fordyce. A local business also was damaged. Propane was accidentally fed into the city water system.

Exploding toilets no joke in Fordyce

So kids, remember that the next time you try to fool Dad with that exploding toilet gag.

From the "It's all relative" department:

Firefighters Larry Patterson and Jenny Lindgren look over the wreckage of a house under construction that was blown down by gusts Wednesday that reached 60 mph. No one was injured. The house is at 14656 Pratt St. in Woodbridge.

High winds cause minor damage

"Living proof that international politics is a Mickey Mouse business" department:

World leaders remember Hirohito

UPI

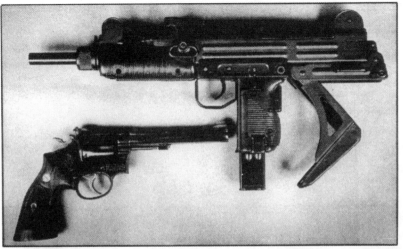
Kenneth P. Lambert/Journal

Moth control plans detailed

Wouldn't it be safer to just buy screens?

COME STAY
WITH US
SPECIAL
RATS

Copyright Houston Chronicle. Reprinted with permission.

Gee, do you think
Mickey stayed here
when he visited Hirohito?

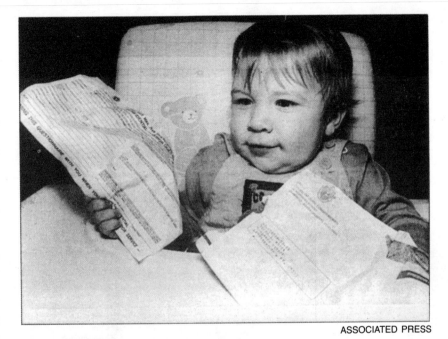

ASSOCIATED PRESS

Jury duty
Tyler Morey, 11 months old, holds a notice to report for jury duty in Berkshire County, Mass.

Hey, it's cheaper than day care.

From the "Exactly how hazy was it?" department:

Thunderbirds Stage
Show At Norton A.F.B.

The U.S. Air Force Thunderbirds perform with hazy skies during yesterday's air show at Norton Air Force Base in San Bernardino.

Iran hangs 70 in drug crackdown

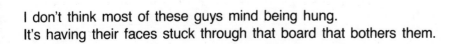

I don't think most of these guys mind being hung.
It's having their faces stuck through that board that bothers them.

From the "How long have you lived at the North Pole?" department:

UPI

Illegal Farm Workers Rush to Beat Residency Deadline

KCC cracks down on gas leaks

From staff and wire reports

TOPEKA — On the heels of natural gas explosions in Kansas and Missouri, the Kansas Corporation Commission on Wednesday ordered utilities to beef up testing for natural gas leaks and replace service lines when leaks were detected.

You can start by closing that door.

Coalition forms task force to combat crime at ATMs

Responding to increased consumer concern about the safety of automated teller machines, a coalition of bankers, manufacturers and trade groups has formed a task force on how to avoid ATM crime.

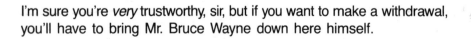
I'm sure you're *very* trustworthy, sir, but if you want to make a withdrawal, you'll have to bring Mr. Bruce Wayne down here himself.

SKI AREA
BOUNDARY

EXTREME DANGER
BEYOND THIS POINT

GOING BEYOND
THIS POINT MAY
RESULT IN DEATH
AND/OR LOSS OF
SKIING PRIVILEGES

Death I can handle.
It's losing those ski privileges
I'm worried about.

OPEN UNLESS CLOSED AFTER HOURS

BIRMINGHAM NEWS

184

© DAVID H. FAUSS, Atlanta, GA

BRIAN MASCK/THE MUSKEGON CHRONICLE

Three-year-old Sam Kushnick's death of blood transfusion A.I.D.S. at Cedars-Sinai Medical Center in Los Angeles on October 13, 1983, and his very healthy twin sister Sara's expulsion from Temple Emmanuel Nursery School in Beverly Hills—not for medical reasons—but because, as one parent put it "the community went berserk," unalterably changed my family's life.

With the publication of MORE HEADLINES, seven years will have passed since that time; a time when pediatric A.I.D.S. was not yet a disease that children died from and when the scientific party line for acquiring A.I.D.S. from a blood transfusion was a "one in a million negligible risk."

Today, the growing pediatric A.I.D.S. patient population is placing a burden on children's hospitals and social service programs already underfunded and understaffed. We are pleased that, through the generosity of Jay Leno, we will be able to continue our support of these organizations.

These books have also allowed me to keep a promise that I made to Sara shortly after her brother's death. She became frightened one evening that she couldn't remember Sam's voice—afraid that that meant she was beginning to forget him. I promised her that night that we would not let Sam be forgotten.

We fervently hope that Ryan White's wish will come true; that this will be the year that A.I.D.S. becomes "just a virus and not a dirty word."

Helen Gorman Kushnick
Los Angeles, California
June 15, 1990